Feck
Per-
fuction

Feck Perfuct-ion

Dangerous Ideas on the Business of Life
By James Victore

Foreword by Danielle LaPorte

CHRONICLE BOOKS

SAN FRANCISCO

To the most beautiful person I have ever met, my wife, my guide and teacher, Laura. Without you there is no me. And no dang book.

To Luca, because I'm pedantic.

To Wyatt and Nova, you are pure love and joy. How did I ever finish this book?

Library of Congress Cataloging-in-Publication Data

Names: Victore, James, 1962- author.
Title: Feck perfuction : dangerous ideas on the business of life / by
  James Victore ; foreword by Danielle LaPorte.
Description: San Francisco : Chronicle Books, [2019] | Includes
  bibliographical references.
Identifiers: LCCN 2018016361 | ISBN 9781452166360 (pbk. : alk. paper)
Subjects: LCSH: Arts--Psychological aspects. | Arts--Vocational guidance. |
  Creative ability. | Creation (Literary, artistic, etc.) | Success.
Classification: LCC NX165 .V53 2019 | DDC 700.1/9--dc23 LC record available at
  https://lccn.loc.gov/2018016361

ISBN: 978-1-4521-6636-0

Manufactured in the United States of America.
10 9 8 7 6 5

Chronicle books and gifts are available at special quantity
discounts to corporations, professional associations, literacy
programs, and other organizations. For details and discount
information, please contact our premiums department at
corporatesales@chroniclebooks.com or at 1-800-759-0190.

Chronicle Books LLC
680 Second Street
San Francisco, California 94107

www.chroniclebooks.com

Contents

Foreword

Danielle LaPorte

James gave us an assignment. Bowls of various drawing utensils were on the table. He passed each of us an article from the *New York Times* to read. There was heavy, thoughtful sighing from the group. *Were we up to the task?* Brows furrowed. Nervous tics were triggered.

When time was up, we broke the silence to present/defend our sketches on racism, privilege, and cultural divides. James was listening, deeply, smoothing the tips of his moustache. And then with equal parts compassion and dagger: "The point . . . ," he said, "is to have a fucking *opinion*."

Point taken.

Because you can't make art without an opinion. You can't teach the world anything without shattering your assumptions. You cannot break free of status quo zombification until you learn to discern truth for yourself.

The anxiety that we normalize, the dulling effect of unquestioned obligations, the thud of "Is this all there is?" when we cross the finish line . . . we don't have to live this way. Just ask the Creatives on the other side. The Fulfilled People. They are not without their agonies—in fact the more woke you get, the more pain you access. But oh, man, the freedom, the depth, the *living*.

Victore believes that normalcy is barbed wire to the human spirit. And questions are the wire cutters. This book is a subversive tool for consciousness-raising from a curmudgeonly mystic who doesn't give a shit what anyone thinks, but who is passionately in love with the world. It's a plea from the heart: Have a fucking opinion and go make something with it.

So inspired,

Danielle

Introduction

We are *all* born wildly creative. Some of us just forget.

As children we are completely free. We can draw and dream and invent imaginary worlds, even imaginary friends. This gift of creativity makes us powerful but also awkward, weird, and vulnerable.

At some point and for various reasons, our weirdness becomes less an asset than a target. We learn to hide our great and goofy qualities in order to dodge criticism and assimilate. We choose not to stand out or act on our creativity. We take the accepted "adult" route, content to be paid for learning rote skills and showing up on time.

In this reality, choosing to accept our weirdness, invent our own future, and live a purpose-driven life becomes a dangerous idea. It's dangerous because it lets the creative beast out of its cage and allows us to see what we are capable of without seeking permission or approval. Dangerous because it opens up the possibility that the life you're living may not actually be yours, but a template assigned to you by scared and unimaginative people. These are dangerous ideas because they challenge your ego, your definition of "normal," your crappy job, and your comfort zone. These are dangerous ideas on creativity and life.

Feck Perfuction is a collection of the lessons I've learned, developed, and followed throughout my career. They come from psychology, sociology, philosophy, and the crazy things my mom said—that have all turned out to be true. These are lessons in unearthing our authentic selves in our personal and professional lives. They are also the mementos that I use to be confident, find creative fulfillment, and get paid for being me.

It is not my intention to be inspirational or make you feel good—but rather to challenge you. I want to ask difficult questions of you, to force introspection and possibly change. I want to tempt you with the possibility that your creativity is not a "weekend" thing, but an integral part of who you are and something that you should start getting paid for—because inspiration without action is bullshit.

This book will reintroduce you to your voice, reconnect you with your weird gifts, and help you find your purpose. Full of stern, funny, and fatherly advice, *Feck Perfuction* tells you things you don't want to hear in a way you want to hear them. It's your guide, your coach, and your cheerleader.

I know from experience that this collection makes for resolutely difficult advice—and is not for everybody. I wrote this book for me, but I hope you find your dangerous self in it.

With love,

Chapter 1. Voice

Your voice is who you are. Maybe not the "you" you carry around every day, but the one yelling from inside, demanding to be heard. Your voice is the way you see the world and how you translate it back. When you train your voice and allow it to grow and be heard, that beautiful sound will carve a path for you to follow for life. Conversely, if you fail to use your voice, others will be in charge of it. And you. Never give in, never surrender. Your voice is your most powerful tool.

01. Your parents were wrong

Parents are amateurs. I mean no slight to parents or to amateurs; I am both. But, growing up, we are given only a few options as to our future path. Either we're told that we can be anything we want, even president. Or that we are to follow a predestined, familial path with a title like MD, PhD, Dr., or Esq. These ideas aren't necessarily wrong, but they are misleading. Your purpose on this planet isn't to become a millionaire, build a 401K, or even get a good job—your purpose is to figure out who or what you are. If you can do that, everything else is frosting. The great oracle herself, Dolly Parton, tells us, "Find out who you are and do it on purpose."

Classically this is called "knowing thyself." Admittedly not an easy task. Many of us are presented with a track to follow that may not be our choice. Just because you were born on a farm doesn't mean you were born to *be* a farmer. In my hometown, two fields were popular (meaning you could possibly make a living at them): nurse or prison guard. I felt no attraction to either. My calling was for the arts, but I disregarded it because I was told it was something "talented" people did, and I didn't want to grow up to be a "starving artist." But the creative urge proved too strong—and painfully obvious—so I chose to ignore the critics, and to fight and sometimes fail in order to see my vision through. I still do.

You can't ignore your DNA. The worst thing you can do is deny who you are, try to be someone or something you're not, and live a life bent and molded by others. As Oscar Wilde put it, "Most people are other people. Their thoughts are someone else's opinions, their lives a mimicry, their passions a quotation." Ouch.

You can be a musician, an accountant, or a sexy, powerful, creative beast—but you have to be yourself first. You have to follow that star. Others without the grit and guts will have to be satisfied with becoming president.

02. Have a damn opinion

There's an American gospel song with the powerful refrain, "This little light of mine, I'm gonna let it shine." We all have that little light. It's lit by our upbringing and our childhood. It's our history, our travels, the things we love, and the things we fear. Our little light is our opinion—and it begs to be illuminated.

Sadly, most of us don't let our light shine, for two reasons: It's too *easy* and it's too *hard*.

It's too easy because it's "little." It's familiar to us. We pooh-pooh our own opinion and don't see the value of what we have to offer. After all, "Who'd be interested in me or what I have to say or my voice?" It's too *hard* because once we acknowledge it, we have to trust it and share it with the world, and we live in fear that someone may not like it. This is a completely valid fear, because the truth is, not everyone will love your voice. But this division is how you define your audience, how you find the ones who will love you for who you are. If you play it safe and choke back your real voice, you are like a rudderless ship, taking directions from the waves.

Your voice is the story you put into everything you do. It's what sets you apart and makes you and your work memorable. It frees you from following trends or begging for ideas, asking, "What do they want?" Now your most powerful tool is asking yourself, "What do I have to say?"

The things that made you weird as a kid—make you *great* today.

03. The things that made you weird as a kid make you great today

When I was a kid, I was full of wordplay and jokes. I loved to sing loudly and poorly. My best talent was entertaining my fifth-grade friends by drawing naked ladies. They looked more like lumpy potatoes, but my audience didn't care. Unfortunately, my level of energy and enthusiasm lacked appreciation at home or at school. I was called "creative"—and it was not a compliment.

As kids, we're all weird. We have our interests and activities, and we like to run them full throttle. As we get older, we realize there's a price to standing out, so we shrink from our weirdness in fear of anyone finding out who we really are. Being weird or different—even creative—should be not a source of shame or embarrassment but a torch to be held high. Weird is about the courage to be who you were born to be. Nerdy, goofy, fidgety; these are strengths. These are gifts! The things that made you weird as a kid are the source of your character and creative powers. These are the base elements of who you are. Not perfect. Not trying. Just yourself. If you hide them, you risk never knowing what you're capable of.

Professionally, weird is a benefit. For some fields, it's a damn prerequisite. Any "successful" actor, chef, musician, athlete, or comedian, when asked what contributed to their success, will answer, "When I was a kid . . ." Pop-culture icon and astrophysicist Neil deGrasse Tyson remembers looking up into the night sky as a child and says, "The universe called me."

When you accept your weirdness and believe in your gifts is when things get really weird. That's when your cause inspires others. When people see their own struggle reflected in yours, you create the potential for shared humanity. Your weirdness speaks to them. That's when you find those people who accept you precisely because you're weird and different. Ultimately you'll hear that glorious refrain: "Oh, you're weird, too? I thought I was the only one!" This is how you form relationships and businesses. This is how you find your audience.

Accept it: You're weird.

I teach the visual arts, but I push my students to understand that what their work looks like is less important than what it says. I want them to express an opinion in their work, to divulge something personal. Their plaintive cry is usually, "If it's personal to me, how could anyone else understand it?" My answer is, "What interests you, interests others." What is most particular to us, even though it may seem personal in its details, can have universal meaning and value to others.

George Lucas grew up in a small, conservative California town but yearned to be a filmmaker and loved racing cars. These three themes—(1) a young man in a repressive society, (2) escape to a better world, and (3) racing hot-rod cars—all form the story line of Lucas's first three major films.

THX 1138 (1971) takes place in a dystopian future where the young hero, THX, yearns to escape the confines of his state-run society and does so in a stolen Lola T70 race car.

American Graffiti (1973) takes place in our not-too-distant past in a small California town. It's the story of two young men on the verge of leaving home for college and a more exciting life. One of the film's "characters" is a yellow 1932 Ford coupe with the license plate "THX 138." And the actor Harrison Ford plays a charming rogue driving a black hot rod 1955 Chevy.

Stars Wars: A New Hope (1977) takes place "a long time ago in a galaxy far, far away" and features young Luke Skywalker, who yearns to escape his small farm and seek adventure. He eventually teams up with a charming rogue played by Harrison Ford, who pilots what is essentially a hot rod called the *Millennium Falcon*. The references to THX abound throughout the Star Wars saga, as names of droids and labels on ships. Even the ubiquitous movie theater sound system Lucas helped develop in 1983 is called THX. Lucas didn't have to look far or invent themes to write about. He never went searching for stories to tell or vehicles to carry them; he just had to look inside and tell his own story. The themes and details he drew on were already very particular to him, but now they have meaning for us.

A less Hollywood application looks like this: A young guitar player doesn't ask marketing to run the numbers to see what kind of song to write. He falls in love with a redhead and is moved to write a song for her. We, in turn, love him for it.*

The common thought is to rely on trends, fashion, or whatever the going mode happens to be in order to communicate. Most marketing and advertising tries to appeal to a wide swath of the population by hiding behind what everyone else is already doing, by consciously *not* taking the lead. But what appeals to everyone is oatmeal. What works for a wide audience is prepackaged, easy to digest, and thoroughly bland.

---

*Later, the redhead breaks his heart and he writes an even better song.

The only thing you learn by following the herd is that the view never changes. You never learn how to express your own truth or beauty and never find out the power therein. You never get to know who you are or what you are capable of.

The more vulnerable and authentic you can be in expressing your opinion, the deeper the connection you have with others. This is the *value* of your opinion—what is most personal and unique to you is the very thing that, *if* you risk expressing it, will speak volumes to others. The hardest part is to trust that your story and opinions have value.

Your struggle with your weight, your love of bugs or rocks or fixing old motorbikes—any passion is a legitimate starting point. Trust your voice, your opinion, and put it in your work. Let it shine.

05. You don't fit in

All my life I've heard the same refrain from teachers, friends, and family: "Why can't you be . . . normal?" What they are really trying to say is, "You don't fit in here." Hell, I agree, I don't "fit in." Not only because I don't want to, but because I *can't*. I just wasn't born that way. It's literally impossible—barring a full frontal lobotomy—for me, or you, to behave like anyone else. There are times for a little "get-along-go-along" social lubrication, but as I see it, "fitting in" denotes a lack of character.

Humans are social creatures. We want to belong and want people to like us. It's natural to want more friends, more customers, and more attention. But when we have to change who we are to achieve that goal, problems arise. We begin to sell off the parts that made us different or special in the first place. We lose our authenticity and our voice. People follow leaders who have something to say and who stand for something. When an individual or enterprise has nothing to say, they're no longer leading but following.

Knowing that you don't fit in is your first glimpse of greatness. It's the first step toward understanding your gift and finding your creative potential. You weren't born to fit in, ready to accommodate every relationship, every situation, every client. Don't contort yourself to fit into a box or a square or a cubicle. The world has enough safe, bland, dull crap.

You are an artist and a genius. Don't fit in. Don't even try.

you are an artist and a genius the problem is that no one informed you of this.

06. You become who you pretend to be

This idea has been around for over two thousand years and has been said by everyone from Ovid to Kurt Vonnegut. The first time I heard it was from my high school track coach. Coach wanted a few of us to train on the local university's indoor track—a luxury forbidden to townies. When we reminded him of that rule, he just said, "Act like you own the place." Acting! Why didn't we think of that? We had to cop an attitude—coach said so! In pretending to be brave, we became brave—even if for a short time. This is a practice that has served me well throughout my career.

Your attitude creates your reality. With the right attitude, you can become who or what you want. It comes by having faith in yourself, your ideas, and your abilities, and by saying, "I can do this. I belong here." By consistently leaning into your fears you create a new way of addressing them. You create a new habit. These habits change your reality. It's not about "faking it" or presenting a false exterior, but rather, through practice, creating a positive attitude of being. This practice becomes a habit, this habit becomes your life.

After all . . . it's all just theater.

Habits
are human
nature - why
not create
some that
will mint
gold?

—HAFIZ

07. Work is serious play

Play is an essential part of life. It's through childhood play that we learn about ourselves and the world. But about the time we exit puberty, we're told to put away childish things. It's time to get serious and get a job. Something that pays well. The fact that we should actually love or even like said job doesn't even come up in the conversation. Thus furthering the dreadful idea that work is just something we do to make money. In pursuit of adulthood, we join the Working Dead, spending most of our lives at jobs that financially sustain us, but are less than satisfying. To continue to develop as humans, we need play in our lives—and not just on the weekends.

Every job—especially every creative job—has two parts, an Objective and a Subjective. The Objective is to satisfy the commercial request: sell the product, attract customers, do what's asked of you, get the job done. The Subjective is the much more engaging—but often left out—ingredient of play. It's *how* you sell and *how* you attract customers. For example, a chef can cook food that's hot and good, fulfilling the objective. Or, through play and imagination, she can stimulate the mind, surprise and delight, even create lasting memories. Play serves both the creator and the audience.

In teaching creativity, I often have to remind students to play, or at least give them the permission to do so. This is why I ask students to make 100 sketches on one idea. This process forces them to plow through all of the logical, usual answers to get to the good stuff. It frees them to make mistakes and entertain the illogical and the wrongest answers. Maybe a crazy idea is not so crazy. This practice helps students become adept at generating ideas faster and unlocks a wealth of possibilities. Their ability to play now becomes their professional shorthand to creativity.

New and innovative work comes from the unexpected places, not the "right" answer, and it's our childlike sense of wonder, curiosity, and play that makes it possible.

"A computer in every home? Balderdash!"

Creativity is dangerous. Not creativity as decoration—the perfect mauve wallpaper to match the couch—but creativity as inventing and pioneering. It's University of Oregon's running coach Bill Bowerman ruining his wife's waffle maker to create "waffle" shoes for his athletes. This was the beginning of Nike. The X-Games sprang from hooligans skateboarding in dry backyard swimming pools and young tricksters pushing the limits of what snowboards, bicycles, and dirt bikes could do. Even NASCAR has its roots in running from the police. Today's dangerous ideas include self-driving cars and privateers planning missions to Mars.

Creative thinking challenges the rules and norms—the way society works. It's the New chafing against human nature's habit of questioning and rejecting anything considered new. Every creation signals the death of what came before. Creativity is change, and change is both inevitable and natural. You can fight change, but it won't end well for you. Or you can choose to accept it and grow with change.

Creativity produces dangerous, wrong, and illogical ideas that lead to a better and more sophisticated tomorrow.

Creativity is dangerous because that is its job.

you a

we

you're

I had a young protégé. He wanted to be a screenwriter.

But his father encouraged him to be a bricklayer, like himself. It was his "lot in life," his father said. "The arts don't make money, bricklaying is a decent wage, and the world needs bricklayers. You'll be one like me."

For 10 years my young savant laid bricks and swallowed his dreams. One day his father's best friend died (presumably from laying bricks). At the funeral the father got up to read a eulogy he had written. My friend was moved to tears. Not by the eloquence of the good-bye—but by the realization that his father was a writer.

Chapter 2. Fear

Your biggest fear is not spiders or sharks—it's you. It's the fear of expressing who you are— lest someone actually see you. Our instinctual fears are a healthy mechanism, keeping us safe; but professionally, FEAR = STOP.

What's stopping you from achieving your goals is not a lack of knowledge or talent and certainly not other people; it's your own fear. Your job in life is to overcome yourself every day. Make fear your BFF, stay on course, and keep moving forward.

Dragons are real. Heroes are real, too. We all have dragons, but we're not all heroes.

Like the children's books say, dragons guard the reward, the wealth, or the love the hero seeks. If we want the reward, we need to face the dragon. For most of us, our dragons aren't physically embodied as wings and scales and fire. They're actually worse.

Every morning, my dragon curls around my shoulders and quietly snarls into my ears, "Failure, failure, failure." I'm reluctant to face it. It's easier to accept the idea of failure—to accept that I'm a failure—than to do anything about it. It's easier to stand down, stay in bed, and not risk failure by not risking . . . anything. This tactic doesn't make the beasts go away; it makes them bigger.

At some point in our lives, we all hear the call to action. Our heart tells us, "This is our time! Seize the opportunity! Carpe diem!" Then we're struck with the vastness of the task: "I gotta do . . . *what*? (Gulp!)" Opportunity demands we take chances, stretch our limits, and grow. But fear grips us, and we become reluctant.

To take a great photo, you have to get into the action. To lead people, you have to stand up and speak. To start a business, you have to risk everything, including making a fool of yourself.

My own dragon never leaves me. He's there every morning, despite having been defeated numerous times. Even after achieving new levels of personal success, I still have to face him. Heroes are the reluctant ones with the courage to face their dragons. Every damn day.

12. The success of failure

When I was a kid, I worked winters as for the National Ski Patrol. Being a ski patroller sounds glamorous, but it actually involved a lot of waiting. To amuse myself during the downtime, I taught beginners how to ski. More often than not, what began as simply learning a fun sport would slip, twist, and slide into an emotional shit show. Skiers want to ski; they don't want to fall. Falling is a big part of the ski learning curve, but mounting frustration and snow down your ski pants does not lead to progress. I quickly learned that if I wanted to actually teach people to ski, I had to first help them deal with their feelings of failure when they fell.

We hate to fail. It makes us feel like we've done something wrong. But by putting yourself in a position to fail—on the ski slope or in your business—you've done something very right.

The first step down any path is most likely failure. Most great tales of success begin rather grimly. Failure is a teacher—just not always the kindest teacher. Its lesson is to not quit and run in the opposite direction, but to learn from failure, to follow its lead. Failure is a test. Its purpose is to weed out those of us who don't want things badly enough. It presents a choice—you can stay down or you can get up and try again. Failure is a shepherd who's smarter than you.

Because of our reluctance to accept the hard lessons of failure, most of us fail even bigger—and don't even know it. We slip into a mediocre life. We quit our goals, lose our "crazy" aspirations, and choose the "easy way." The consolation prize is a flat screen TV and a bag of chips. From the outside, this looks like success, but it's actually settling for less—comfort disguised as success.

The path to success is marked by failure. Not just once, but again and again. Accept it and learn. Reject it and . . . well, fail. I still teach beginners how to ski, and my best lesson is still, "If you're not falling, you're not skiing."

We all want freedom in our lives. We want the freedom to grow, experiment creatively, and design nimble and flexible lives. We want the freedom to do the work that's in our hearts and get paid for our gifts, not just our ability to punch a clock. We want the freedom to explore, play, fall flat on our faces, and do it all over again.

All we need in order to create this magic is for someone to give us permission. So, we wait for a savior to unchain us from our desks and grant approval of our freedom. We wait for some defining moment in the future, but only when circumstances are conducive, of course. "After I make a few dollars, lose a few pounds, pay off my debt . . . *then* you'll see!" But circumstances are never kind, and permission never comes.

No one gives you freedom. It is not earned or doled out over time. You take it, through bold and brave moves. Freedom is a leap. It's taking the jump and believing that you'll land safely, or at least won't die. It's the reward for putting faith in yourself and your voice. There's no warden or shining knight; the only person qualified to give you your freedom is you.

take it.

14. Tombstone

A few years back, after one of my more impassioned lectures about DIY culture and seeking new opportunities without the safety net of a client, a young buck in the back row raised his hand.

"Mr. Victore," he said, "I hear what you mean about taking risks in your career . . . but I've got rent to pay." I was more than a bit shocked by his defeated attitude, saddened at how the practicalities of life had already beaten this young soul down so hard that his biggest ambition in life was to satisfy his landlord. Gone was adventurous youth. The kid was no longer the hero of his own life. He had no fight in him. His future flashed before my eyes—beer gut, sheepishly waving a white flag out the window of his minivan, his life getting smaller and smaller.

"What's your name?" I asked.

"Thomas," he said.

"Thomas, here's your tombstone: 'Here lies Thomas. He would have done great work, but he had to pay the rent.'"

I don't advocate reckless selfishness or throwing all professional caution and considerations to the wind. I myself have a number of people dependent on me for their livelihoods. But what example am I to my children if I give up all hope and sell my dreams? I serve my family best when I am happy, excited about my work, and getting paid for my creativity. I want my children and even the public to see me fighting for my living and my freedom, not begging for it. This is certainly not an easier route, but undoubtedly it's a better one. And one with a better epitaph.

15.

Beware

Flac.
Plati
OVER
Photo

id

tudes

STOCK

raphy

16. There ain't no rules

Kids love rules. Play a game with any five-year-old, and they'll ignore the actual rules of the game but create their own. Then they heap rules on top of those rules—making it up as they go along. Then if the rules don't work in their favor, they change the rules.

This is not such a bad idea . . .

Adults love rules. We actively look for them, and use them like a handrail to find our way around. We want to know where we stand. We seek structure to our floppy lives, so we ask, "What are the rules around here?" What we find are actually just strong suggestions of what you can and cannot do to fit within polite society. These are not really rules, but society's habits, handed down and unconsciously agreed upon so everyone can play nice and avoid mayhem. When we do splurge and break the rules, we feel as though we've gotten away with something—when in actuality we have only taken what freedom was ours to begin with. Most rules are an invisible fence; they exist because we believe they do.

The problem with the rules is that they're generally unisex and one-rule-fits-all. They promote conventional, business-as-usual thinking and don't allow for the concepts of individuality or play. Rules like "Stay within the lines," "Don't rock the boat," and even "Be nice" seem innocuous enough but are creatively stifling.

Even in the commercial practices of architecture, film, theater, and business, there are rules about how things are done. Only when we see those rules beautifully ignored do we come to a new, higher realization of what is possible.

The rules are fine for some, and, like the boundaries of a playing field, they serve a purpose. The problem starts when they begin to fence in your spirit. While it's not necessary to totally disregard the rules, it *is* critical to have your own set to live by. Rules that not only allow you to call BS on the existing standards, but also give you the elbow room and flexibility to lead a profitable, creative, and meaningful existence.

Make your own rules, make your destiny.

THE RULES

5.
~~8.~~ NEVER WORK FOR ASSHOLES

2. FIRE (BAD) CLIENTS

3. NO SMOKING

4. GO FOR LONG WALKS

1 ~~5.~~ TREAT OTHERS as (YOU) would like to be TREATED.

Feck
Perfuction

17. Feck perfuction

People are too concerned with the idea of perfection. We crave it at an ironfisted-control-freak-Martha-Stewart level in our lives. And we nearly kill ourselves—or let others kill us—pursuing it at work. Perfection is a head game we play with ourselves—no one outside of our heads really cares about the nitpicky details we stress over. It works like this: Set unobtainable goals; then, when you don't achieve them, drive yourself into depression. You can give it a fancy name like "True Perfectionist," but I prefer "Self-Hating Narcissist."

On its surface, perfectionism seems like it would be a professional advantage, a creative accelerator. But really, as a driver, it hits the brakes more often than the gas. Perfectionism stops you from starting projects—or even relationships—because you are not ready. It stops you from finishing projects because they are never quite right. "When it's *perfect*!" is our defense, but this habitual overthinking leaves us stymied, unable to get over ourselves and just move.

Should you strive for excellence? Of course. Pay attention to the details? Yes. But never let "perfect" stop progress. You know what's better than perfect? Done. Done is better than perfect.

My father was an active man. He had a full military career, built a business, built the house I grew up in, and helped my sisters renovate theirs. He was always moving. When he was 60, he was diagnosed with Parkinson's disease. Over the next 15 years, he remained as active as he could while the disease slowly took hold of different parts of him. Eventually, he was confined to a wheelchair, then to bed. Through all of this, he never complained. He never once asked, "Why me?" He was—and still is—the strongest man I know.

Everything about your life is a test. All things, both good and bad. They are a test of your character. They test whether you can accept challenges with grace and then grow because of them, or whether you choose to whine, curse the fates, and let your anger spill out, tainting everything and everyone around you. Obstacles, fear, the naysayers: These are all just tests of your resolve, of how determined you are to succeed.

Life is a test of your conviction and vision. You choose whether to play the victim or the hero.

19. Your ego can't dance

Weddings are a test, not only for the bride and groom but also for everyone else. At some point, the music builds and there's a cue: "Everybody *dance now!*"

But not everybody dances . . . cuz it's a test. It's a test of how comfortable you are in your skin. Check my wedding math: If half of the guests get up and dance, more than half of those are mummies. Their bodies are stuck in a fixed, dancelike position, encased by the fear that moving will expose the dancing fool trapped inside.

Everybody can dance. To hell with the music; just let go and move.

What stops you is your ego. It doesn't want you to look bad or funny or goofy. Dancing is goofy.

Your ego starts to develop when you're a child and is influenced and shaped over the years both by you and by society's reaction to you. Its purpose is to protect you by controlling you. Like a gyroscope always reacting and rebalancing, making sure that it's on top of the situation, your ego is in perpetual motion to keep you from feeling shame or embarrassment. It's not bad, it's a part of you—but it's not all of you. Your ego wants you safe, but safety isn't interesting or fun or creative.

To be freely creative is to be completely and honestly *you*, not a sphinctered-down version of yourself. Worrying what others may think is the death knell of creative work. You have to be willing to make a fool of yourself, or at least go out on that ledge. Creativity wants to let go of control and to present authenticity and vulnerability. This is what moves others. This is attractive. Complete conviction makes great work.

I have a good pal who is possibly the worst dancer in the world but loves to dance. When he's on the dance floor and flails his leggy body, he becomes the Lord of the Goofy Dance—and the crowd goes wild! It's no surprise he's also a brilliant filmmaker. Make the work you want to make, dance like a fool, and leave your ego at the door.

The prominent Jewish scholar and philosopher Maimonides wrote, "Teach your tongue to say, 'I don't know,' and ye shall progress." The Jewish religion places a high value on education and knowledge, so where does this line come in and why do we care about it? Unlike the majority of our everyday thoughts, "I don't know" is uncertain; it's admitting to ourselves our frailty, humanity, and humility. We are open to *not* having an answer—and certainly not having all of them—so we are free to receive input. Admitting you don't know is the path to knowledge and even wisdom.

Creativity comes from this space as well. Creativity presumes nothing. "Reality" is a suggestion, and we live in a cartoon world where everything and anything is possible. Freed from concrete restraints, we can enter a creative state of not knowing, open to all opportunities, all answers, all realities—a world of questions instead of rote, knee-jerk answers. When we allow ourselves this childlike view, we're open to a rich universe of imagery and ideas to play with. Questioning is the definitive tool for creativity.

My pal Richard Wilde runs the design department of the School of Visual Arts in New York. Every year he asks his students a simple question: "Is there life on other planets?" The majority of their responses have to do with percentages of possibilities vis-à-vis numbers of stars, something Carl Sagan said, and a lot of other bullshit. Only those open and honest with themselves are able to say, "I don't know." This is the only true answer.

21. The wrongest answer

As a communication designer, my job is not to communicate. I want to make your head explode. My primary objective is to make strong, surprising, and memorable statements that teach, inform, inspire, or even confuse. To do this, I have to ignore logic and stop making sense.

The American artist Edward Ruscha devised a simple rule for distinguishing between bad and good art.

Bad art makes you say, "Wow! Huh?"

Good art makes you say, "Huh? Wow!"

Looking at bad art is like eating fast food. You're excited about the thought of it, but when it hits your stomach, the relationship ends quickly. Good art is seen, but not immediately understood—"Huh?" Then comes the "Aha!" moment when the subtext, the real meaning, unfolds and our mind expands. Comedy also uses this principle. A joke sets up a logical story, lets you formulate what would be the obvious ending in your head, then destroys the original premise with an alternate and, hopefully, humorous ending.

The visual arts are an intellectual field, and the visuals we use are the teaspoon of sugar that helps get larger ideas across. There are pathways to communication and understanding other than the brain—the heart and the groin are both equally good. You don't have to feed your audience information they already know in a way they already expect. Play with their senses and tease their rational way of thinking. Trust your audience's curiosity. Whether they confess it or not, the public wants to be intellectually challenged, not spoon-fed a common, boring, or "right" answer. To surprise and enlighten your audience is to give them a gift.

My mentor and friend Henryk Tomaszewski summed up this idea beautifully: "All my life I've tried to find signs that everyone can understand. A designer's work comes down to a continuous search for new associations, symbols, visual paradoxes, the construction of deliberately wrong, illogical areas. This game demands a sharp eye and an infallible perception, but it also involves getting the message to the viewer. And sometimes you miss."

22. The struggle is everything

The ancient Indian text the Bhagavad Gita tells the semihistorical story of a civil war that took place in India approximately 3,600 years ago. It's also an allegory to explain the fundamental truths of life, growth, and spiritual evolution. The battle is a metaphor for the ongoing struggle between the light and dark forces of nature. As the story opens, we find our hero, the great warrior Arjun, slumped down in his chariot, riddled with fear and anxiety—and with way too many questions. Luckily for Arjun, his charioteer is none other than the Hindu god Krishna in disguise, who spends the next 18 chapters in a prolonged discussion with Arjun, teaching him about life and death.

I first read the Gita in my early twenties, when I was just starting out in life. I found the story more confusing than enlightening. One line, in particular, stuck in my craw. Krishna tells Arjun, "You are not entitled to the fruit of your labor— only the labor itself."

I was perplexed. Why couldn't I have the fruit? I was working hard for it. I wanted fame and notoriety. I wanted to get paid so I could buy crap! This was *why* I worked. I wanted it—and I wanted it now, dammit! I wasn't doing good work for the pleasure of it; I was only concerned with the fruit it would bear. The reality is, I suffered, because I didn't understand.

What time and patience have taught me is the truth of that beautiful line: If you focus on the reward, you'll never be happy. The fruit—the money, the fame, the whatever—will never be enough. Even further, focusing on the reward means *not* focusing on the work. The process becomes secondary, and we learn to hate the process. We loathe Mondays and thank god for Fridays. Our daily lives become the dullness between paydays.

For great artists, writers, scientists, the process of creation *is* the reward. The process of learning and growing, and all the intermittent victories and defeats are the reward.

Learn to enjoy struggle. The reward will take care of itself.

Chapter 3. Start

In the long process of rising to greatness or even goodness, starting is the hardest. It's a commitment, and like all commitments, it's scary. Partly because when we start it implies ownership. Our journey becomes . . . real. It's like jumping out of an airplane with a parachute that you have to trust; there's no going back. But you can't see the world without crossing an ocean, so just start. That first step is a doozy.

Most people start by stopping. An utterly genius idea pops into your head—start a business, write a story, quit your crappy job—and you let it die a death of inertia. You fail to start. This makes complete sense; as Newton's first law tells us, an object at rest—like your ass—tends to stay at rest.

For any creation, any new project or new move in your life, starting is the hardest part. Too many of us are waiting to start. But while you are waiting, others are already living the life you want—the only difference between them and you is that they started. There are no special instructions, and no one is standing in your way but you. Don't think, don't rationalize, just do. Start and don't stop—cuz momentum is your friend.

all
BEGIN-

nings
are
Hard

I've got no idea what I'm doing. I never have. I started my career at 21—the day after I was asked to leave art school. I was ill equipped, unqualified, and unsure of myself. I wasn't ready, but I moved forward anyway. I had a goal, and my excitement and fear carried me.

Nobody is ever ready to begin. We want a few practice rounds—not for realsies, just a warm-up to get started. Bad news: You'll never be ready. You'll never be fully prepared, and the conditions will never be perfect. You'll never have all your pencils lined up or all your ducks in a row. You'll always feel uncertain about what you're doing or what the final outcome will be.

You just have to start. Waiting till you're ready is a form of self-sabotage, a good excuse to quit while you're behind. Experience is great, and practice has its place, but boldness makes way for action.

As for me, there will be new situations and unexpected moments that I won't be ready for—and I still don't know what I'm doing, but that's never stopped me before.

1. READY

3. FIRE!

2. AIM

26. What is success?

Growing up, our parents, teachers, and friends paint a picture for us of what success looks like. It is usually exactly as advertised on TV—the mad scramble for moneyhousejobmoney. Were this brainwashed version of reality true, the world would be populated solely by accountants and bankers. It would be a bleak and dull world with no room for the misfits, artists, and creators who form our culture.

While that mundane vision of success is what most people seem to want, you need to ask yourself, "What do I want?" Just as the first step of any journey is deciding where to go and how to get there, our first step should be to define success for ourselves.

This is imperative early in your career, but even on down the road you need to pause, check your progress, and realign your priorities by asking yourself a few important and sometimes difficult questions.

Are you following a passion?

Do you have time for friends and family? Health and spiritual nourishment? Study or travel?

Is your work a service to others?

Is your work emotionally fulfilling?

Basically: What do you cry about in the shower?

Setting your own terms for success is how you form a purpose-driven life. Without these standards in place, you live the clichéd life, passive, unfulfilled, and on the losing end of compromise. You surrender the pursuit of happiness to chase a paycheck.

Along your way to happysuccessville, there are many choices. Choose love. And always choose "you."

In Yiddish, it's called "chutzpah." In English, we say, "grow a pair." Call it what you want—spunk, swagger, confidence—assuming success is an attitude adjustment that follows after a physical adjustment.

All emotions have a physical counterpart. When we win big, we assume the Ali-looming-over-Sonny-Liston pose, our arms raised in a triumphant V. When we fail, we hang our heads and curl up in a ball. It's hard to be confident while lying in a fetal position.

The verb "to assume" has three main meanings: (1) to suppose to be the case, without proof; (2) to take or begin to have; and (3) to take on. For you, I mean all three.

Assuming success is feeling successful—in your walk and your posture—*before* you succeed. The idea is to proactively alter our posture to invite the positive attitude and outcome we desire. By using a powerful, dominant body stance, we produce positive changes in our behavior. There is, of course, scientific backing that may or may not prove this phenomenon, but I don't care about that. Just fucking grow a pair.

Success isn't a dot on your lifeline that you hit at age 40 or age 65, before immediately retiring or dying. It's a process that has a very definite beginning—right now—and depends on how you carry yourself at every point along the way. It's a conscious choice to feel successful that you breathe into your character. Do not wait for success to saunter into your life; there is no papal anointment or secret handshake. It's a done deal. Congrats. Welcome to the club.

28. Have a plan

At 19, I had a plan: move to New York City, go to art school, open a studio, and become the best poster designer in the world. I gave myself 15 years; it seemed a reasonable amount of time.

How I was going to achieve these goals I had no idea, but I had the big picture . . . The rest I'd just make up.

Life doesn't always follow a plan. As the French say, "Shit happens." Failure was not in my plan. Being asked to leave art school was not in my plan. Losing my day job wasn't either. But none of these were deterrents. I had a plan. Having a plan helped me form—and keep—a vision of the long term. Having a plan gave me conviction.

At 35, I had kicked the stuffing out of my plan. I had far surpassed my goals. I was an accomplished, in-demand designer with solo exhibitions around the world. I bought a SoHo apartment, married, had a kid, then a house—all the milestones of success. Then a funny thing happened. I woke up at 40 and found myself floundering professionally and failing miserably at life. I realized I no longer had a plan—my plan had ended five years earlier. I had forgotten to re-up the plan.

These days I teach "having a plan." I often sound like Barney, the purple dinosaur from TV, spouting childish platitudes like "You can't score without a goal." But, seriously, you can't.

In interviews, I ask my young charges where they see themselves in 10 to 15 years. If they answer, "Working," I ask them to be more specific.

A plan isn't writ in stone. You don't have to check it every January 1, and you certainly don't have to be so manic as to check it every morning and adjust it before bed.

A plan is your true North. It keeps you from wandering aimlessly through life. You now have a quest. It helps define what is and isn't you. It gives you parameters of what you will and will not do, jobs you will or will not take. More than anything, your plan is a vision of who you can be and an acceptance of the idea that you are worthy of a beautiful and meaningful life.

Have a plan.

29. Improvise

In short,

Retool and get back at it with no loss of vigor, traction, or enthusiasm.

Remain steadfast and resolute in your goals, but be flexible, ready to make it up as you go or to scrap the plan altogether.

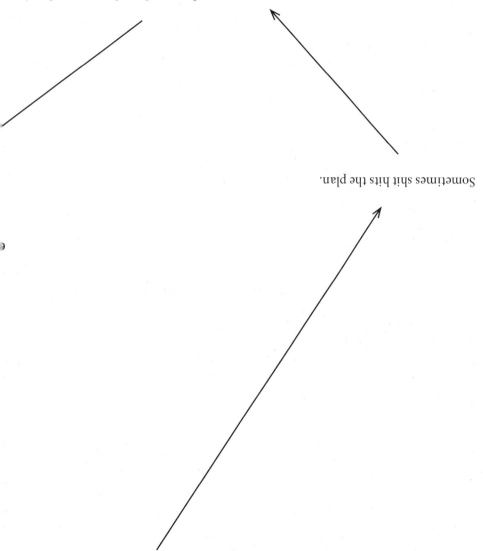

Sometimes shit hits the plan.

Having a plan is great, but don't fall in love with it.

30.

Change the
World.

start
small.

start
NOW.

31. The first rule of business

I often ask students what they think is the first rule of business. Their answers are uncertain, more like questions themselves, and sound like something they gleaned from their fathers. "Profit?" "Stay in business?" "Service?" All good rules, but not the first rule. My first rule is possibly the most irresponsible, unreasonable, and impractical business advice I have. That's why it's brilliant.

The first rule of business is *fun*. Why fun? Without fun, there is no commitment, no enthusiasm or energy for the hard work ahead. Long hours are a drudgery and perseverance in the long term is shaky. Fun is knowing how to play and incorporating joy and wonder into your work. It means being open to mistakes as innovation and reminds us that we don't *have* to work, we *love* to work. Without fun, you are merely one of the Working Dead, going through the motions, loitering for a payday.

My own father would cringe if he heard me impart something as hedonistic as, "If you don't love what you are doing then don't fucking do it." But fun is as important as profit and service in business. It also makes those things possible. If you love what you do and have fun with it, that feeling translates to your customers. We are moved by people who put personality into their service—and take our business away from those who do not. Going into business or following a career does not mean that you leave behind joy and play—it means you now get paid for it.

- have ~~fun~~ ~~for~~ ~~a~~ ~~little~~
- ~~just~~ ~~do~~ ~~time~~ ~~in~~
- ~~find~~ ~~something~~ ~~you~~
  ~~can~~ ~~do~~.
- ~~it's~~ ~~something~~
  ~~not~~ ~~about~~
- ~~save~~ ~~your~~
  ~~something~~ ~~el~~

- have FUN. ~~_____~~

Years ago I had a young assistant named Chris.

Whenever a new project came into the studio, the first thing Chris (being a newbie) would ask was, "What do *they* want?" I found this an odd question. Of course, a client wants to attract as many hearts, minds, and dollars as they can, but what Chris wanted to know was: What did the *they* want from *us*? How the hell do I know what a client wants? I'm not sure what *I* want most of the time, let alone what the world wants or what will sell.

We have no control over the needs, emotions, or tastes of other people. Even with all the market research and focus groups in the world at your command, pinpointing what will make them happy is still a guess—an expensive guess. My guess is that the world wants you. It wants your weirdness. It wants your complexity and screwball perspective. It wants your opinion, your humor, and your history. It wants all that's beautiful and powerful inside of you.

Don't waste your efforts trying to please other people. Make work that is meaningful to yourself first. Create work or a business that reflects your genuine passion. Your enthusiasm at the cellular level creates excitement and energy that radiates outward. You become a beacon, attracting your people, your tribe, your audience, even clients.

I work to make myself happy. This makes my clients happy. More importantly, it makes their audience happy.

33. Confidence is sexy

I've got a cousin named Tony. Tony's a fireplug, barely five feet tall and well over 200 pounds, but everyone loves him. I mean *everyone*. Anywhere we travel together, there is always someone there who knows him and is ready to buy him a drink. Beautiful women flock to him. Tony is not rich, not particularly good-looking. Tony's gift is confidence.

Confidence is not something we're born with. It's more a habit than a hardwired personal quality. It is not bestowed like a gift. And for most of us, it's not easy.

I was shy most of my life. As a kid, I was told by authorities that I was shy, so I assumed that position. Not until I became a professional did I realize that my shyness was not a trait that would serve me well. I frequently find myself onstage or in front of a camera and have to play someone who is comfortable being there. Years of practice have lessened my fears, but I still have to summon the courage to walk confidently to the podium. My confidence is not something I walk around in all the time, but I can call upon it in short bursts when necessary. Confidence is one of those ambiguous traits, like willpower or intuition, that can be practiced, exercised, and strengthened like a muscle.

My definition of confidence is "being there." This means being in the moment and acting with intention, not distracted by second thoughts or being "in your head." It means just moving forward—confidently. It means accepting the self-doubt and fear that tend to run (and ruin) our lives.

Confidence comes from a mind-set of abundance and wealth and gives us the freedom to ask for help, to ask for more, and to ask for what we deserve. Confidence makes us attractive to friends and clients. It gains trust and even inspires confidence in others. Confidence is damn sexy.

34. Excitement breeds excitement

Everything vibrates.

This is a simplified description of the quantum field theory, which basically states, "Everything in the universe is made up of energy vibrating at different frequencies." This includes you.

We all vibrate at different frequencies or volumes, from 1 (low energy) to 10 (high energy). Some even go to 11. That idea alone should stir up the universe inside of you. This information means that it is entirely possible to raise someone else's energy by using your own. Puppies do it all the time.

I was having coffee with a new client, a lovely and talented guy. He was feverishly chatting about his life and goals. His eyes were lit up—hell, his whole face was lit up. I was becoming excited to be a part of his program. But when we got down to talking about his product and marketing ideas, he suddenly became just another business exec, dull as dishwater. The light left his face. I said, "Wait a minute, where's the other guy? The exciting one?"

If, in the effort of bringing people to your cause, you feel like you're selling yourself, please stop. No one wants to read your sales bullet points or hear a canned elevator pitch you handily memorized. And absolutely no one wants to read your newsletter with well-selected stock photos. It's not about persuasion. You can't trick someone into loving you. It's all the energies vibrating inside of you that people are attracted to. Your excitement breeds their excitement. This even translates to the product and the things we make. These become infused with our energy, magic, juju, or mojo, whatever you wish to call it. We tend to choose one item over another because "it speaks to us."

This vibrational theory works for gaining an audience, showing your work, building teams, and especially teaching. Let everyone know that you are on a quest, and help will come to your aid.

When you share your vibrations with the world, you start a wave, and everyone gets caught up in it. The Beach Boys call this "Good Vibrations."

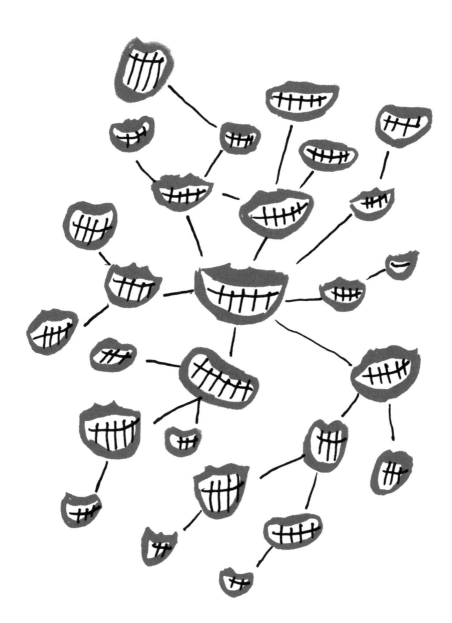

35. The cost of freedom

Everything has its price. Greatness includes the cost of the struggle and the weight that that label holds. Conversely, bowing to your circumstances and not aspiring to better carries the burden of unfulfilled ambition. It is important to understand the costs early in your career, when you are most susceptible to outside influence. This foresight allows you to stay on target.

At 19, I moved to New York City to fulfill a dream of becoming a poster designer. Once there, I quickly found that there was no actual position for that job title—so I had to make one up. I also had to accept the cost of that dream.

With my first poster, *Celebrate Columbus* (1992), I sought to use my skills as a designer to comment on social, cultural, and political issues and to make a difference. It was the five hundredth anniversary of Columbus's discovery of America. New York was gearing up for parties, celebrations, and a grand Fifth Avenue parade. Now, I was no expert on Native American history. My grade-school education covered the important highlights of Plymouth Rock, the first Thanksgiving, and Captain John Smith. Thankfully, Disney filled in the facts about Pocahontas. I also seemed to remember reading about pox-infected blankets and the broken treaties and systematic genocide that continue to this day. This side of the story needed telling, and I was going to do it. Crowdsource-funding websites were not around at the time (heck, the internet was not around at the time), and I had doubts about finding a client to fund my opinion. Nevertheless, I pressed on and used my own funds to professionally print and wheat-paste 5,000 posters around New York City. The only money I had was earmarked to pay rent, but I was on a mission. I was not going to let poverty or my landlord stand in the way of greatness. This get-'er-done mentality was admittedly a bad business plan, but it served its purpose at the time.

The recoil of spending my rent money was that I could not pay rent—for a while. Consequently, every few weeks, the doorbell would ring. Waiting there was a man in a suit. "James Victore? You are served," was his only line as he handed me an eviction notice. At the time, I was embarrassed. I threw the papers away. Now I wish I had kept them—these legal notices were proof of my conviction, the price I had to pay to make posters. My girlfriend, who was living with me at the time, did not like receiving eviction notices. She, too, became the price. Today I continue to happily pay the price that aspiring to greatness demands. Luckily, my wife does, too.

Celebrate Columbus 1492-1992

América hoy, 500 años después / America today, 500 years later / L'Amérique aujourd'hui, 500 ans plus tard

Chapter 4. Action

Fear paralyzes you. It shrinks your sphincter, constipates your thinking, and stops all movement. The antidote to fear is action. Acting on your thoughts and intuition is where the rubber meets the road. Movement is the key. Big, bold, and forward. Keep inventing, keep making, and keep imagining your future. Make your life happen by acting on it. And once you start, you better keep going.

The world is brimming with would-be authors, dancers, and entrepreneurs full of bright and innovative ideas, holding the future of creativity inside them. Most of their ideas will never make it to market and their talents will remain silenced. The biggest reason for this is too much thinking and not enough doing, too much worry and not enough *action*.

Success goes to those who keep moving, to those who can practice, make mistakes, fail, and still progress. It all adds up. Like exercise for muscles, the more you learn, the more you develop, and the stronger your skills become. Success is about action. Action beats worry. Action beats thinking. Action always wins.

You can't be a mover and a shaker if you're standing still.

37. Love, attention, and consistency

Healthy, steady growth doesn't just happen; you have to plan for it.

When my first son was a toddler, I bought a house in upstate New York. The house was fairly secluded except for a view of one other house. Wanting my privacy, I decided to plant a row of trees: 33 four-to-five-foot-tall pine trees. I knew nothing of planting or growing trees, and I didn't have to—my crazy Uncle Joe did. Joe was the head groundskeeper of a ritzy country club nearby and a mad floricultural genius. He taught me everything he knew about the planting and seasonal maintenance of the trees. He even guaranteed that if I followed his instructions, "These suckers will grow a foot a year. Same for your boy." What Joe was slyly hinting at were the universal applications of his plant-based philosophy. Systematic and strong growth—for a garden, your business, your children, even your Instagram following—comes from love, attention, and consistency.

They say if you *love* your work, the rest is easy. I say there's still a lot to do, but love makes the efforts and late nights and extra duties worth it. Love gives your work a purpose. It also guarantees that you'll still care for your work when TSHTF.

"Multitasking" merely means doing a number of things poorly. This is why we pay *attention*. Focus on one thing. Sometimes this approach is called "Do one thing and do it well." Read, study, and practice to become an expert on your subject.

The third of these three traits, *consistency*, is the most important—and also where most people fall off the wagon. Ask yourself every day, "What am I doing today to make way for growth?" For gardeners, making way for growth means knowing when to plant, mulch, and feed, when to water and when to prune; and doing this season after season, year after year. For parents, it means being consistent with your messaging and your demands; children need to have structure and to know their boundaries.

In business we must have a plan, get the word out, follow the numbers, know our brand, and, more importantly, stay "on brand." I have seen countless businesses succeed not because they were genius ideas, but because they continually followed through on their plans.

Love the game, focus, and follow through. All three facets help growth happen. If you skip one, the process falls apart. If you don't love what you're doing, following through is difficult. If you can't pay attention and be consistent, don't fall in love.

38. Seek the muse

The muse is an ethereal goddess rumored to be the source of our creativity and inspiration. These figures are so popular that everyone has their own creative source on demand and their own private way of connecting with her. Some tell tales about the muse visiting during long walks along the beach. Others have to hunt her down and wrestle the truth out of her. Yet others say that she is a myth, that the only true enlightenment is found by hacking away every day at five a.m., and that our only salvation is work, work, work. There is no definitive answer on the existence of the muse, how to find her, or how to go about translating her instructions. The most common knowledge about the muse is that she won't find you at your desk, in an office, or on a schedule.

She presents herself to us unexpectedly, when we are unaware and in an open state, able to be influenced. She comes to us in the shower, and at the gym; exercise seems to release congealed thoughts and free the muse.

My own goddess frequents pool halls and dive bars—at least that's where I find her most often.

The reason so many wonderful ideas and beautiful sketches are born on bar napkins is that you are *in a fucking bar*, not at your job, not trying, not working, not forcing your brain through a grinder. Your sense of mirth and play are in an altered state.

Only when you step outside of your routine will chaos, madness, and life-changing opportunities find you. Yes, work, work, work; but get out and wander, too. All work and no play makes Terpsichore a dull muse. Go! Seek inspiration, open yourself to her gifts. Avail yourself of the gods and set the conditions so that they may whisper in your ear.

Just remember to bring a pen.

39. Run from comfort

Once upon a time, one of my mid-career students came to me with a bleak look on his face. He told me that as he returned to his apartment the night before, he'd had a massive and unsettling realization: He hated his job. He worked in a scholastic publishing house where, he said, everyone else was equally unhappy.* That evening, he walked into his apartment and saw, smack dab in the middle of his leather sectional couch, an ass divot—directly across from the TV. He realized he was a prisoner of his comfortable apartment. Locked in by a decent mortgage rate paid for by a cushy job . . . golden handcuffs and all. "I like my apartment," he said, "and now I'm stuck."

The search for comfort and security rarely yields the desired fruit. We want the easy way, but the easy way is a trap. Complacency is the enemy, and settling down is settling. Our desire for an easier life gets us stuck in a smaller one, judging everything by the comfort and ease it brings, not by what it costs our soul. We willingly kill time "just chillin'," while the muscles of our instinct and intuition grow flabby. We've got games, toys, and instant messaging but are spiritually and emotionally empty. We look around the internet and ogle others' creativity but put off developing our own. The search for meaning is replaced by shopping on the weekend. Even our food is calorie-rich but nutrient-weak.

The answer is to burn it all down and trust that you can build a better, roomier life.

In 1962, President John F. Kennedy gave a speech backing the NASA Apollo effort to land a man on the moon: "We choose to go to the Moon in this decade and do the other things, not because they are easy, but because they are hard; because that goal will serve to organize and measure the best of our energies and skills, because that challenge is one that we are willing to accept, one we are unwilling to postpone, and one we intend to win."

Today the idea of doing something because it is hard seems as dated as the Apollo program. But hard work, such as the struggle to find a fulfilling job, benefits our souls and forms the core of our grit, fortitude, and character. This is the hard work of self-discovery. By age 35 or 40, many of us reach a plateau, not the moon we initially shot for. The day shift is not you at your best. The uncomfortable spot is where your true voice is: shamelessly and outrageously *you*. The brave ones—companies and individuals—who risk comfort and safety for a chance at beauty and meaning have the potential to attain more—to actually move someone.

*I can't even think of the bad karma passed on to our kids.

Religion played a large role in my youth. Catholic school, altar boy, catechism, the works. During Sunday church service, there was a hymn that I was particularly fond of and would sing loudly: "Seek and ye shall find, knock and the door shall open, ask and it shall be given." Being an imaginative kid, I would act out this possibility in my head; I would find a big door in the clouds and knock, and from behind the door angels would appear with gifts—like a heavenly trick or treat.

Despite this invitation from god, asking for help has always been difficult for me. I was raised to be strong and independent, never in need of any assistance. Asking for help meant I was weak, stupid, or ignorant. It's taken me a few years to learn that my thinking was wrong and even backward. Asking questions is the path to knowledge, and asking for help is how you progress.

No one goes it alone. You have no archenemies planning your demise. The world wants you to be happy and to succeed. Ask for help. There are people who have made the journey before you. Reach out to them. Like angels with gifts, they want to share their knowledge and help.

41. Hold the line

Admit it, you're a caretaker. You say yes to solving other people's problems for a number of reasons;
- To avoid taking care of your own shit
- To pacify and avoid conflict
- To control every situation and make everyone happy
- To be liked
- To prove your loyalty (again) by taking on more work and longer hours

Most of us feel that saying no at work will initiate a sequence of events starting with losing our job and not getting paid, and ending with social banishment, cat food on crackers, and eventually a lonely death in a trailer park. And heaven forbid saying no to family—they'll stop loving us forever.

So, we say yes when we mean no.

The cost of all this yes is that we begin to lose ourselves. We slowly lose our personal time and even our self-respect. We end up angry and resentful of our job or loved ones, all because of one lousy habit of saying yes.

The gentle art of saying no isn't about shirking work, friends, or society, but about becoming a better contributor, a more worthy, equal, and happy partner. Bragging about how much time you spend at work shows a complete lack of commitment to your life. Saying no lets others know that you have boundaries and standards. It means taking a stand for yourself.

I am a happy designer because over the years I have crafted creative ways to say no to my clients. We are both better for it. I understand what they want, but if I don't agree with their demands of me or my time, I am free to offer alternative creative solutions. If I feel that our relationship isn't respected, I am also completely free to fire them and walk away happy. The result is that I no longer feel like a victim, constantly on the losing end of compromise. When you say no, you hold the line for your self-respect.

Stop putting up with others' crap that doesn't serve you or propel you to a higher calling. Draw a line—and hold that line for yourself and as an example for others.

If you do what's expected of you and accept what life has to offer, the best you'll get is high blood pressure and a beer gut. As Rosalind Russell says in the 1958 film *Auntie Mame*, "Life is a banquet and most poor suckers are starving to death!" Or, as my mother used to say, "If you don't ask, you don't get."

You gotta ask for more. I've taken this advice to heart and created a professional habit to ask for more—more time, more creativity, and *always* more money. Asking is hard, but the universe is wealthy and happy to provide for those who make the effort to ask. If you don't ask for more, all you get is a paycheck. You'll never be satisfied, and it will never be enough.

Dream big—if you want a pony, ask for a unicorn.

43. Accept less

In Jane Wagner's 1985 Broadway play, *The Search for Signs of Intelligent Life in the Universe*, the disenchanted career gal, new-age feminist, wife, and mom, Lynn, groans, "If I'd known this is what it would be like to have it all, I might have been willing to settle for less." Like Icarus, she realizes that what she wanted isn't what she wanted. Lynn's struggle to follow the herd led her to crave money, success, power, and popularity. True then, true now.

We want creative freedom and agile lives, yet we attach ourselves to the very things that restrict our movement. We spend an inordinate amount of energy doing and acquiring whatever it takes to achieve the modern idea of success—and our roving eyes always want something else. Our storage units are stacked high with the shit we want, but don't need. We make career decisions based on our fear of poverty or what others will think, and we follow the pack because everyone else does. Left with no elbow room to seek our creative potential, we throw up our arms in defeat and say, "I can't chase my dreams now, I've got a cable bill to pay."

We buy the sales pitch that these things will bring happiness along with them—only to find out later that what we really desire are simpler values—values in the form of love and acceptance and being heard.

If you want more in your life, you may have to accept less. Accepting less means less clutter and less meaningless stuff. Less distraction, less servitude to work, less debt, less greed, and less craving. It means surrendering our attachment not only to physical things, but even to our past and the possible future.

Your happiness shouldn't teeter on a bank ledger or come from any source other than acceptance of who you are.

Never settle and never give in, but accept less.

44. Kill your phone

We live in a culture designed to distract. Screens dominate our life. We work on screens. There are screens in our elevators, schools, and taxis. We carry screens in our pocket for the times between other screens. We even have smaller screens within our screens.

Emails, chats, texts, pads, pods, and clouds have become leashes jerking us out of our quiet time. They demand our attention, leaving us no room for solitude or deep thought.

When I was a kid, there was a time and a place for a phone call—the phone was nailed to the wall. Now, it's all the time, including at the dinner table or on the john (seriously?). We hand our distraction down to our toddlers when we give them our phones to amuse and babysit, so they, too, become incapable of handling boredom. The new tools have made it too easy for us to get sidetracked from the meaningful experiences of our lives.

Our brains are being rewired, our etiquette forgotten. We're learning new habits but sadly forgetting the powerful instincts we were born with. We now trust our senses, memories, and gut feelings less and put all our faith in Google. These bad habits rot the discipline necessary for contemplation or study and rob us of the grit necessary to follow through with long-term goals.

This is a technology problem and an addiction problem. As with any addiction, we need to take charge of it in order to stay committed and reach our goals.

Craft takes concentration, excellence takes time. To be serious about our work, we must be conscious of the time we spend on ourselves versus the time we spend on screens.

Make your life easier. Kill your fucking phone, and save your soul.

I sign my work. I always have. My design heroes signed their posters, book jackets, and ads. It's not done out of an inflated ego, at least not in my case. I do it to express confidence in my work.

I have an English pal, David, whose dad was an electrician, or a "sparky," as they were called. As a kid, David occasionally went out on calls with his father. Once, while he was finishing up a large fuse box, his dad reached in and signed the inside of the box. "Why did you do that?" David asked. "Artists sign their work," came the reply.

The point here is about taking pride, ownership, and responsibility for your work. If it's a good job, "I did this." If there's something amiss, "I did this." Our reputation is all we have, and our signature should be a mark of that excellence.

Today David runs Hiut Denim out of Cardigan, Wales. Every pair of jeans that comes out of their small factory is signed by the master craftsman who made them—because artists sign their work.

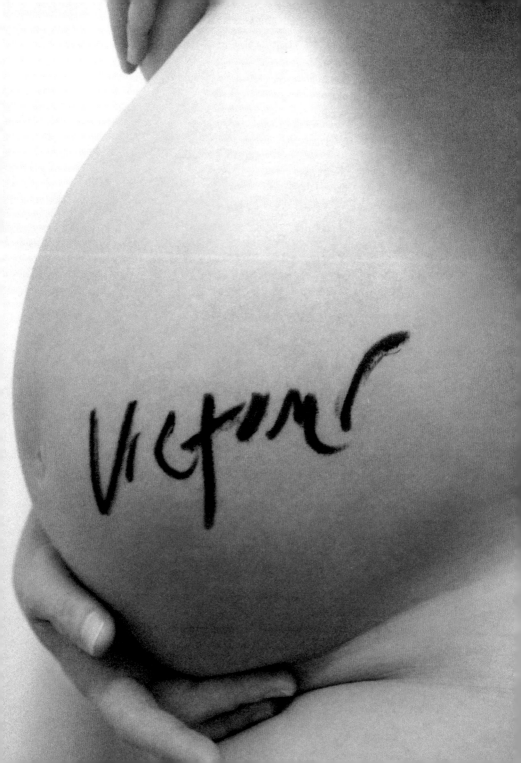

46. Do the work

I hate doing the work. I don't want to wake at 4:30 a.m., beat the sun up to steal the time to write. I don't want to make a plan, check the details, and follow through. Sacrifice, patience, and perseverance are not my strongest traits. Nor do I want to be optimistic and have faith.

But I have to. I gotta do the work. No one is going to do it for me.

Perhaps if I do all the petty little bits and do them well, these efforts will become habit. Maybe all these little actions will start to add up. Maybe I can become good at these things and in time build a better version of myself.

I don't know, I just do the work. Every damn day.

I zig when others zag. Like any entrepreneur, I love the excitement and activity of framing out new ideas and then making, creating, and promoting it all. I've got side businesses on my side businesses.

I love being busy, but it's easy to get caught up in the frenzy and confuse mere business with real growth. I have to occasionally check myself and make sure that I'm creating healthy business practices, and not just hacking away at life with a dull blade.

I took the idea of "sharpening the ax" from a saying attributed to Abraham Lincoln: "Give me six hours to chop down a tree, and I will spend four hours sharpening the ax." The attribution is erroneous, but the sentiment still stands—it's about taking the time to prepare before you make the work.

This preparedness includes developing our crafts, skills, and hobbies. We also need rest and introspection to replenish our energies and stay productive.

But the real preparation is to become students of our lives. To continually develop ourselves by staying curious and always learning.

The hustle and the daily grind can wear you down. Fuck the hustle. Find those things that promote the proper growth and expansion of your life and work. Slow down, read, study, replenish your soul, and sharpen the ax.

My wife and I make love every morning—with coffee.

Each morning, whichever of us prepares the coffee, or has the foresight to fix it the night before, also leaves the other a note. The notes are usually quick, collaged or drawn, or just a groggy sticky note. What it looks like is less important than what it says.

Coffee notes are small reminders to not take our love for granted. They're also a daily practice, getting better at making statements of devotion to an audience. Here it's an audience of one.

As commercial designers we sometimes get caught up in our love of the craft and in the myopic details of color and form. We forget that we work for a public: real human beings who are hungry for an honest, truthful voice. People who deserve our attention, our love, and our best work. Whether it's for a worldwide campaign or an audience of one, I want all my work to be acts of devotion, like coffee notes.

Inspir-
ation
without
ACTion
_____
is

*And vice versa.

Chapter 5. Habits

Nothing shapes us as much as our habits. The way we move, the way we speak and eat and even think, these are all habits picked up along our trip, and we adopt new ones every day. Some are useful, some are not.

Most habits are unconscious, ingrained by mere repetition, and hard to shake off. But you can get good at anything. Start forming new habits that will shape your professional practices, and gain a positive attitude and perspective about who you are and where you need to go—not where your un-conscious acts and thoughts take you. These, too, can be trained, shaped, and made strong by steady practice and awareness. Take an inventory. Pick and choose which habits to keep and which to ditch. And maybe add some good ones.

We all have critics. You can hardly make a move without bullies, haters, or your family voicing an opinion on it, ready to point out your mistakes and elbow you back into the fold.

But there are crueler critics than your friends or society, inner voices that cast doubt over your career and life choices. Voices that steal your determination and replace it with fear and flaws.

Mine sound like my dad.

Where your attention goes, you go. If you focus on your flaws, they'll flourish right in front of you. Your work will pale in comparison to others'. Your life will be less shiny. If you look for trouble, you'll find it; and the critic will always be right.

But the critic isn't right. You are not wrong or weak. Judging yourself is a waste of your time and energies—and quite frankly we are bad at it. As critics we are unduly harsh on ourselves and we pay attention to the wrong things.

To kill the constant, nagging thoughts of failure, we have to be defiant and take command of our lives and our choices. We have to focus on love and gratitude toward ourselves. We have to focus on our gifts and talents. Kill the critic and get back to work.

FAT
Dumb
Poor
ugly

We pre-shit on ourselves so others won't. We joke about how fat we are while trying on new clothes, or pooh-pooh our talents before sharing our talent. We hide our insecurities under a "cheeky" sense of humor.

Self-deprecation is healthy when it means being humble or witty, but continually calling yourself a loser becomes self-sabotage. You ruin the experience of *you* for others.

This goes for compliments too. We don't believe 'em, and can't accept 'em, so we poop on 'em, right in front of the giver. Like the cook who apologizes for the meal before you've tasted it. She may as well just spit in your soup.

Words have power. The problem with repeating negative mantras to yourself is that you start to believe them. Then others believe them.

Watch your words.

52. Brave and scared shitless

On a hillside, two generals astride their horses are quietly reviewing a battlefield. It is clear to both that they're outnumbered and outgunned. The first general calls to his aide, "Lieutenant! Get me my red shirt!" After a moment the second general, perplexed, asks, "General, why do you call for your red shirt?" "If I am wounded in battle, my men will not see the blood and they will continue to follow me into the gunfire." The second general thinks on this for a moment and calls to his aide, "Get me my brown pants!"

As an emotion, bravery never runs solo. It always has a chaser of fear. No firefighter, athlete, daredevil, or speaker at the podium is actually courageous without an equal dose of cowardice charging through them. You can be brave and scared shitless at the same time. As a matter of fact, you have to be. Bravery puts you into the game; fear keeps you from doing something *really* stupid.

Your fear should never keep you from doing what you need to do. It's just a reminder that it won't always be easy. It's also a reminder that that's the way life works. With courage comes fear. With change comes reticence. *C'est la guerre.*

The next time you need to ask for more money, move up in rank, or present your idea to the clan, remember that the fear you are feeling may have a little bravery mixed in it. Leave your brown pants at home.

53.

Comp

is No

Conv

lain in g
t
ersation

54. The secret of the universe

The best advice I ever received was on a dirt track in New Jersey. As an avid racing enthusiast, I was attending a motocross school. We were practicing the "hole shot," the start of the race where anywhere from 4 to 40 riders start from a standstill and, in a full throttle sprint, try to be first one through a bottleneck turn.

Being more greenhorn than expert, I asked the coach which gear I should be in when I reached the apex of the turn. His matter-of-fact answer was, "The right one." It took me a moment to figure out he wasn't blowing me off or being a smartass. His answer was that he didn't have the answer. He was telling me that I had the answer. I just had to trust it.

The secret of the universe is that no one knows shit. No one has the right answer, because no one has *your* answer. We want to know. We seek answers in books and seminars. We look for guidance from teachers, heroes, gurus, and even the internet. We've gotten so used to looking around that we've stopped looking inside.

Success is measured in hindsight. Any advice from those farther down the road comes in too neat and easy a package. Their success came from their own trials, failings, and messy blunders—and their ability to keep going. Everyone is making it up as they go; some just fail more successfully.

You can model yourself after others and even emulate the 10 Things Millionaires Do Before Breakfast, but ultimately what will work for you is practicing, taking chances, and learning to trust your own answer.

No one knows which gear to be in. I suggest trying them all.

I'M NOT REALLY SURE.
WHA...?
WHAT DID STEPHEN HAWKING THINK?
GO ASK YER MOTHER.

55. The second arrow

Shit happens. That's the first arrow.

I held class at nine a.m. on Tuesdays at the School of Visual Arts, an admittedly difficult time of day for 20-year-olds. Inevitably one student would storm into class fresh from a life-threatening experience—they missed a train or were bumped by another passenger. There they were, indignant, still raw from the unfortunate event, holding on to their shock and anger. By indulging their inner baby, they let the situation ruin their day and pissed in the pool for everyone else around them.

Life happens, and we react. *How* we react is a choice. We can choose to let life beat us up by letting our emotions run off leash, by blaming, or by striking out. Or we can choose to let it go and walk away.

According to a Buddhist parable, the second arrow comes from our own hands. It hits when you beat yourself up. We all make mistakes, bite off more than we can chew, or fall into debt. The idea is to be conscious of these mistakes, apologize to ourselves immediately, and move on, improved from the experience. Mistakes, accidents, and crappy days are part of the process. Suffering is a choice.

56. Beautifully flawed

My son, Wyatt, has a crooked smile. He was born with hemi-facial microsomia, a common birth defect in which the lower half of one side of his face is smaller than the other. This "medical condition" makes him very cute.

We all have our dents, details that make us feel different, inadequate, or even ugly. We want to hide from them and hide them from the world, but they're our best parts. People are attracted to imperfections. Your large and crooked nose, the gap in your front teeth—these make you sexy. Your flaws, quirks, and extra curves make you stand out. Lead with them.

The same goes for your work. Most creators aspire to some ideal of perfection but usually land closer to boredom. Only when we see Frank Gehry's architecture do we realize that boxy buildings are bland. In my own work, it's the mistakes, the extra hairs in a brush stroke, or the clumsy lettering, that people applaud.

We are all flawed, and yet somehow we are all perfect. My son will have a choice about how he sees his asymmetry, whether it's his misfortune or an opportunity to find his voice. We can drown in our flaws or, by owning them, we can find our strengths.

Pob

Ne

ody's
*
fect.

*Not you. Not Pobody.

58. You've got a big but

Like you, I should be creative, rich, and happy, but I've got a laundry list of excuses. I would be,

> . . . but I started too late.
> . . . but I live in the wrong place.
> . . . but my parents wouldn't let me.
> . . . but I have kids.
> . . . but I have bills to pay.
> Like you, I have a big *but*.

These are all valid excuses, and, as with all reliable habits, we lean on them like crutches—perfectly good reasons to avoid risks and remain unhappy. Our "buts" keep us safe and give us an easy out. Like the fox from Aesop's fable, we didn't really want success anyway. Blame it on your "but."

Still, at some point, you gotta stop listening to your "but." Ignore the reasons you can't, didn't, shouldn't, and won't.

There's nothing standing in your way except your big but.

you have
No.
f riends,
you have
no enemies

you only have TEACHERS

Some people are poison.

You've met them, these well-meaning folk who want to protect you from failure but are actually shielding you from success. In lieu of support, they offer up their own fears: "You're going to start a business . . . in *this* economy?" Or, "Shouldn't you get a *real* degree first—something to fall back on?" Misery just looking for company.

Our own families can be poison, but we need to recognize that they love us—even if they express their love through a film of worry.

Everyone in your life influences you. To make bold moves, surround yourself with people who give you strength and energy. People who, if they don't have solutions, give salves and support. Seek people who are medicine, who are aligned with your vision and ready to champion your struggle.

61. Let go, kitty

When I was a kid there was a popular "motivational" poster that featured a kitten clinging to a knotted rope. "Hang in there" was its maxim. The message was presumably to persevere, keep going, keep on truckin'.

That cat gave the worst advice ever.

Tenacity and stick-to-itiveness are healthy traits, but most of us suffer from hanging on too long to things that don't work, to ways that are old-fashioned, clichéd, and not particular to us. Our fear of the future and the unknown has us holding on, white-knuckled, to our tiny ideas, closed to the expanse of possibilities that life has to offer.

Most of us, myself included, have held on too tightly to repeated patterns in our lives. Addictions that don't serve us and routines that keep us down. Like an annoying older brother smacking you with your own hand, saying "Why are you hitting yourself . . . why do you keep hitting yourself?"

We know what actions lead to finding ourselves right back where we started, surrounded by bad influences and bad habits, frustrated and defeated—again. We're also conscious that we need to break these customs in order to move forward. We need to stop hitting ourselves, let go, and replace these actions with positive, healthier ones. Then we can let these new, healthy acts form our character.

Let go, kitty. Let go of your attachments and your misguided habits. Our preconceived notions of "the way it is" are the source of our frustrations and anxiety; they have us fighting the flow of "the way it might be."

Whatever is going to happen, surrender and let it happen. Let go and let the universe do its damn job.

Chapter 6. Purpose

Most people are lost. Or at least feel lost. It's understandable. We take a job because a job becomes available.

We move passively like leaves in the wind from one gig to the next, making a change only when we're sacked or when the phone rings with a better offer. Not actively pursuing a calling, but professionally aimless with no direction.

The reality is that you are not lost—you're searching for a purpose. A purpose is a reason to get up in the morning. Excited, horny, and ready for the day.

A purpose is the spark that incites you to move, act, and follow through. It provides focus and single-minded determination to get up and kick butt. You ain't lost, you're searching.

63. Love something other than your selfie

By most accounts, the keys to happiness and longevity include the freedom to express your feelings, a sense of usefulness, and friends. Though the modern trend to these goals is through drugs, therapy, or meditation, you may have better luck getting a dog.

Caring for something or someone other than yourself is understanding that there are bigger things in the world than your ego. It's also the beginning of finding a purpose in your life and work.

A purpose gives your life meaning. It's a reason to get out of bed. With a purpose, your life is no longer about you and your needs, but about serving a larger community. It's about making work that matters and that directly affects the lives of others. It's about doing work out of love and a sense of belonging, not because we have to.

The knights, the samurai, the Boy and Girl Scouts, and even the movie-mythic Jedi all have a moral code of decency to live by that centers around serving others. Let them serve as your example. Love something other than yourself. Help, teach, lead, or perform unrewarded good deeds.

Of course, we need to make our daily bread, but when our efforts rarely have any effect on or meaning for others, life can feel like treading water. Financial success is great, but the world doesn't need more millionaires. We need more creative people who give a damn about something other than themselves. You needn't give away all your belongings or move to Bali or India. Start small. Get a plant.

64. Trust as inspiration

As a commercial designer, a number of things excite me creatively and motivate me to make great work: the opportunity to share my creativity with an audience, the novelty of doing a project for the first time, and, of course, getting paid. But nothing ruins a perfectly good hard-on for work quicker than having a client who does not trust me. Trust is the lifeblood of my business, and possibly of any business. It sets the stage for good work to happen. When we fail to put our trust in others, we get standard-issue workplace practices—employees are micromanaged, second-guessed, and made to feel replaceable. Being told what to do and how to do it reduces even creative enterprises to drone factory work.

Similarly, there is no better way for a parent to crush a child's spirit than by restricting their creative freedom and discouraging mistakes. When you trust your employees (or your children), it's encouraging, it's empowering, and it breeds loyalty.

I have a relationship with the Do Books, a start-up publisher that came to me with a long-term project and a small budget. Because of the low fee, I asked for complete creative freedom. Essentially I was asking for their trust. Understandably, this idea scared them, but they agreed to our contract. Their trust inspired me to do my best work. After the first stage of the project was released, they posted this on their blog: "James Victore asked us to trust him, and we are glad we did."

I'd be lying if I said that trust is easy, especially in business. But the easy way is always a trap. Trust me.

Start with
10 simple
vegetables.
Alice Holden

Mo...
B...

to
ho...
O...

DO/
ESIG...
Why b...
is key...
ever...
Al...
B...

DO/
DISRUPT/
Change th...
status qu...
Or becom...
M...hay...

DO/
PROTECT/
Legal advice
for startups.
Johnathan Rees

our and
childbirth
...oline

DO/ BREATHE

DO/
BRE...
Calm
Find f...
Get st...
Michae...
Willian...

Michael Townsend Williams

DO/
PURPOSE/
Why brands
with a purpose
do better and
matter more.
David Hieatt

DO/
PRESE...
Make you...
...n jams,
...tneys,
...kles and
...rdials.

...r
...spire
...hieve
...sible.
...eown
...access

...d your way.
...e a living.
...best self
...nge

DO/
WILD
BAKING/
...re

...Dunk, Jen Goss, Mimi...

65. Trust yourself

My wife has given birth twice by natural childbirth. Not outdoors in a field, mind you, but outside of the traditional hospital setting. Her reasoning was, "My body knows what to do. I trust it."

Trust is a hard issue. Trusting others is a test of your faith in humanity, but trusting in yourself is a total reevaluation of your worth and personal authority. These days it has become easy and fashionable to crowdsource our opinions. We always know the right answer, but we fail to trust ourselves and instead subcontract to strangers. Unless we exercise our instincts, we will never learn to trust them.

The beginning of trusting yourself is merely understanding that your thoughts are in your head for a purpose. They matter, and they are valid. Listen to your own opinions, rather than the nagging echoes of fearful friends and family. Too often those thoughts that creep into our heads are fear-driven, wild prognostications of failure, carnage, and financial ruin, that usually begin with, "What if . . . ?" But where your thoughts go, you go. It takes faith in yourself and your abilities to see these thoughts as the imposters they are. When the fog of doubt is cleared, the imposters banished, we can begin to see more clearly our true nature and instincts. Then, with a little faith in yourself, you can raise your sights, look up from the abyss of failure, and take the next step. Then the one after that.

Trusting yourself gives you the faith that people will hear your message, be inspired by your cause, and rise to your challenge. It's completely probable that not everyone will heed your call; but trust that the ones who do are your team, your support, and your audience.

Your body knows, your instincts know, your impulses are spot-on—don't question, just trust.

66. Judge not

We create because we need to.

The act of invention, giving form or meaning where previously there was none, drives us and makes us happy. We make art or business to suit ourselves—and are often surprised when our talent is acknowledged by others. Our labor touching someone else's heart is a serendipitous by-product of creation, but it's secondary to making.

Seeking others' approval of your work is a common mistake most creators make. Often I receive requests from young designers asking my opinion of their work. My stock answer is that what I think of your work is not important. What's important is what you do with it. What's important is how it makes you feel, how you talk about it, and how you get it out into the world. Not only is it not important what I think of your work, but also, frankly, it's not important what *you* think of it. Most of us are terrible judges of ourselves, let alone our work. We're so familiar with the marks we make that we can't recognize them as unique or special.

You are not qualified to judge your own work, you are only qualified to make it. Don't judge it or call it good or bad. You can only make the work and get better at doing it. No artist or author or inventor in history ever *knew* they were making something of interest. They didn't look for answers, they lived the questions, taking deliberate action every damn day and allowing the answers to reveal themselves when the time was ripe. The proof of their genius could only be found out in retrospect.

You have no idea what the public will like or respond to. The critical or financial success you seek will come from your ability to follow through with the work you love.

This is a radical idea.
When you begin to see
your work as a gift, it
changes why you work
what you make, and
even who you work
for. When your work is
a gift, your goal is no
longer to satisfy a boss
or client—or even to

earn a paycheck. You Now work to make yourself happy and therefore speak directly to your audience. Because you Now give them something of value: A piece of your **self.**

Breathe DEEPLY and Always

68. Health

Any classic motorcycle enthusiast knows that if your engine dies, the three things to check are gas, air, and spark. Make sure it has fuel; check whether the air intake is clogged; and pull the spark plug to see if it's clean, not sooty or corroded. This same maintenance checklist applies to our bodies. We need to maintain our gas, air, and spark.

To keep your motor turning and maintain the fire necessary to do the work at hand, you need to eat healthy food, exercise regularly, and get enough sleep. Most Americans apply themselves to a fairly unhealthy regimen of work, work, work, and more work, pushing their bodies too hard with little or no maintenance. They become overstuffed, fall apart, and don't stop until their bodies force them to. Burnout is not only real, but epidemic.

Watch your intake. It is too easy these days to binge on crap food and forgo exercise. The human body was not designed to run on pizza and beer (I know. I've tried.). Here's a hint: If most of the food you eat is white—you're headed for the pits.*

Learn how to breathe. One of the best side effects of taking a class in yoga or meditation is the reminder of how to breathe. I find myself going through a busy day stealing only tiny sips of air, forgetting how replenishing it is to fill my lungs and fully expand my chest.

The spark is just what it sounds like: We need massive servings of magic, play, and excitement in our lives.

Junk food, no cardio, and a stale sex life make Jack a dull boy.

*Pro tip: Go gluten free.

69. I'm a fake

I am a big fat fake. I suspect you may be a fake as well.

As for me, I've made a few attempts at an education,* read a few books, asked lots of questions, and now (voilà!), I'm an "Artist, Designer, and Writer." Why? Mostly because I said so.

Okay . . . I may occasionally peer over my shoulder, on the lookout for the authorities demanding my credentials and rubber-stamped certificates. But until they come, I press on regardless.

The feeling of being a fake or imposter is rampant. Most everyone is limping their way along, seeking approval of their very being at every step. Even with college degrees, certificates, and medals confirming your existence, it takes confidence, practice, and chutzpah just to feel worthy. There is no license to be bold, and waiting for outside consent will only make you old. You and I don't need anyone's permission to be creative, sexy, or even weird. We just decide to be.

*Failed at one university. Asked to leave another. 'Nuff said.

70. Learn everything

I taught at the School of Visual Arts in New York City for almost 20 years. Most of my students arrived right out of high school. I never thought this was a good idea because they didn't know much. They were going into to a field where their lives and backgrounds and interests would make their work rich. The students who brought gold to the table were the ones who had pursued other avenues first—transfer nursing or biology students or older students going back to school. The ones with a little road under them, who had lived and, more importantly, had failed.

As a teacher it's my job is to invite students to bring their baggage into their work. Without my pressing, a young student may think that there is a right answer to search for outside of themselves. Already schooled by a smorgasbord of television and various media, they end up picking from a very small menu of usual, logical, and safe ideas and visuals, making the obvious more "obviouser."

The best designers are interesting people first. Smart, funny, and curious people.

Here's my point: Learn everything. Then forget it. Let the original details and nuance blur, put your own imprint on the content and action, then create. Get an education. Get some life experience. Amass some skills and interests. Learn about Shakespeare and poetry, about diet and nutrition and woodworking. Japanese flower arranging helps tremendously, as do improv class and aikido. Let all of this come inside of you. Let it steep, becoming your muscle and memory. Then, put it in your work. It may come out as obvious references, or it may just be an added flavor. Or it may just make you happy.

Let all your loves, fears, and interests saturate your work and make it memorable. *Who* you are is the most important part of your work—never leave it out.

Books never mentioned my name.

Whether you like it or not, you're a teacher.

You teach in the work you choose to put out into the world, as well as in your carriage and demeanor. Your lessons are present in how you treat others and how you treat yourself—both the good and the bad.

The best example of this is the way children learn from their parents. They will learn your walk and your weaknesses as much as what you'd like them to learn. "Do as I say, not as I do" doesn't work. Besides sending mixed messages, it instills distrust and lack of conviction. You can't expect greatness from others when all you express is your confusion and pain.

The good news about your new role as a guide is the positive effect you can have on the world around you. The world needs more teachers to share the wealth of their compassion and empathy, their excitement and enthusiasm. Accepting your role as teacher instantly makes you a better person.

Lead by example, see yourself reflected in others, and be responsible for your actions and your legacy.

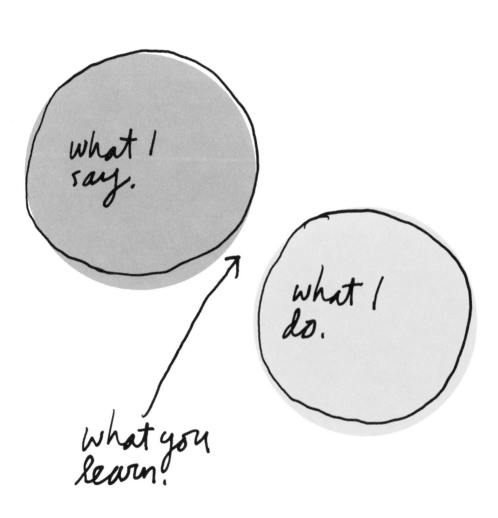

72. For god* or money?

I start every project as a god job: an opportunity to make smart work, reach an audience, inspire, enlighten, educate, influence, entertain—the works. But as altruistic as my own goals may be, occasionally my client does not have the same vision. They would rather opt for a more obvious, club-upside-the-head approach and cut out that "art" crap. Maybe they don't trust their audience's intelligence, or they find safety in mediocrity and don't want to stand out. Whatever their reasons, as their hire, I'm in their world and I acquiesce.

No risk, no glory.

What may have started as a god job slowly twists into a money job, so I cut bait, get paid, take my name off it, and get poised and ready for the next opportunity.

There are some jobs you do for god and some you do for money—and it's important to know the difference. When a decent job turns into a godless job, then get 'er done, get paid, and move on. Don't show it to anyone, and don't look back. You can choose to fight with the philistines, or you can accept the world the way it is and be happy.

---

*My lowercase "g" means no disrespect to any god, goddess, deity, or religion.

On its surface, this advice seems not only irresponsible, but quite frankly un-American.

But while the pursuit of financial gain is a worthy venture, it cannot be the thrust—the "why" of why we work.

Taking on work for money (instead of creative opportunity, growth, or play) is a bad habit that leads to a bad portfolio. Crap work begets more crap work.

Making choices about your creative career based on your fear of poverty is not only shortsighted, but shows a complete lack of faith in your creativity.

Trust the bigger picture. Follow your gut, follow your instincts, and follow your interests. Let money follow you.

74.

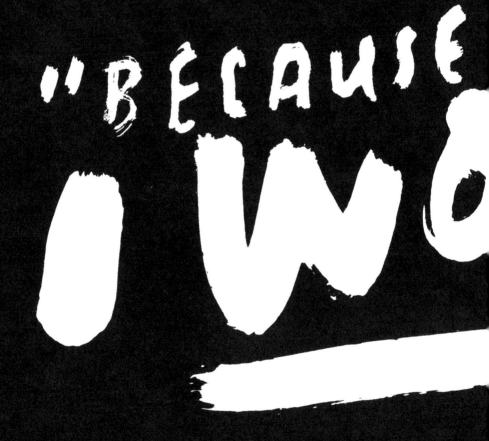

*is the only reason you need.

"You can't change the world, but you can clean up your room."

Like most mom-isms, this one took a few years to untangle. It came whenever she sensed my confusion at the way the world worked. At first I thought it was an admonishment to ignore the facts and get busy with the vacuum. Later I realized it was my mother's way of saying, "Be the change you want to see in the world." Mom was telling me that I couldn't help others or make them happy until I could do these things for myself.

You may call it being the change or leading by example, or just doing your best. But if you want to change the world, you have to start with yourself. Real change starts with your education, your empathy, and your awareness of the world around you.

The better you take care of what is within your reach, the farther you can reach. This is how you affect others. This is how you change the world.

76. A younger me

A few years ago, a colleague asked me to pen a short message to his son on the occasion of his 21st birthday. It was to be part of a collection of advice from his dad's friends, a thoughtful gift to help prepare the boy for the future.

What could I add to this guide that would have meaning and provide comfort? Since the best gifts are the ones we want for ourselves, I only needed to ask what I would say to my own younger self upon entering adulthood. What could have eased my own way and calmed the path?

For both myself and my friend's son, "relax" was my only thought.

Even today, "relax" is the advice I need daily.

I tend to turn life and work into a sausage-making race, grinding everything though a small sphincter and trying to control the outcome. But control is a myth; and, as much as I try, life refuses to be wrangled—and trying to wrangle it ends with me fighting myself.

Relax and trust the process, trust the stars, and trust yourself. Let everything happen to you in its course, then take a deep breath and relax.

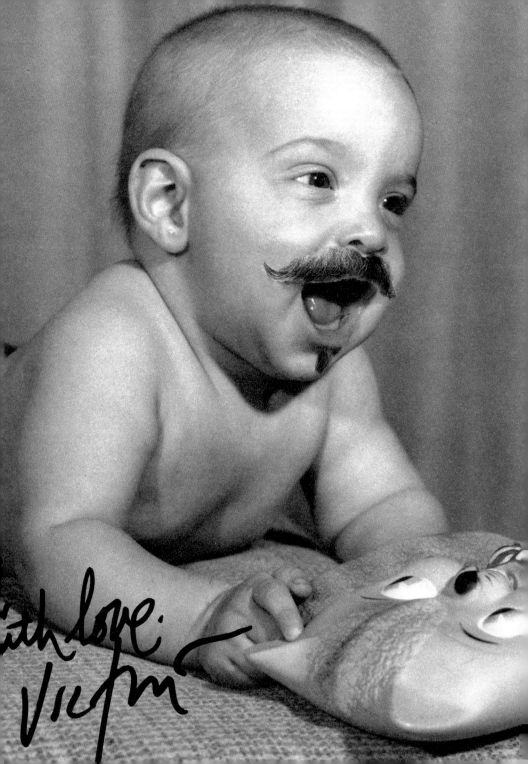

With love,
Victor

make
work
mat

that
ters.

Acknowledgments

I will be eternally grateful to Bridget Watson Payne for plucking me from the crowd and smoothing out the book process.

To my agent Lisa DiMona, thank you for your wisdom and guidance, and for fielding all my harried questions, but mostly for your friendship. Excelsior!

A humble thank-you to my most capable and trusted editor, Mirabelle Korn, for collecting the rubble of my words and reassembling them into English.

To the entire staff at Chronicle Books, hey, let's do this again sometime.

To Danielle LaPorte, a beacon for so many: Thank you for your gracious words and thoughts. You have snatched the pebble from my hand.

Thank you to my friend and designer, Jason Bacher, for his vision, guidance, and humor in the form, shape, and content of this book. And for his good fucking design advice.

To Laura, the most perfect muse.

Special thanks to Chris Thompson, for sharing his courage and calm and wisdom with me.

A genuine thank you to Bob and Cherry, for the elbow room and freedom to write this book. And, of course, for the brick.

I am grateful to David Rhodes and the School of Visual Arts for allowing me to practice and develop my craft under their roof for so many years.

To my chairman, guru, and friend, Richard Wilde, always an influence.

A big thanks to Paula, Carolyn, and Arlyn, you make the wild machine work beautifully.

To all my past students in various classrooms, events, and coaching who worked both with me and against me to help forge these ideas.

To my friend Paul Sahre, the hardest-working man in the design game, thank you for your patience with all the fits and starts I put you through with this one.

To David Hieatt and Miranda West for keeping me in the book game. And for trusting me.

To all the bars and restaurants in Brooklyn and Texas that granted me office space, keep the tip.

Lastly and always, to Joe and Rosalie Victore for the strength and humor that has always saved me.

Credits

25 Hafiz. *The Subject Tonight Is Love: 60 Wild and Sweet Poems of Hafiz.* Translated by Daniel Ladinsky. New York: Penguin Books, 2003.

27 Image courtesy of Nuts Watch Co., Japan, 2009

42 Photo by Zack Minor

79 Image by Alexander Gardner, 1872, *Celebrate Columbus*, Offset, 35.5 x 23.75 in, 1992

95 Photo by Christa Meola

105 Image by Joseph Decamp, *Pauline*, ca.1907

111 Image courtesy of NASA, Universe: NASA 7993119, Andromeda galaxy, Center: MSFC, Date created: 1978-12-01

115 Photo by Bruce Soyez-Bernard

133 Image courtesy of The DoBook Company

155 Photo by JCPenney